The Addison Collection

The Addison Collection

John W. Newton

RESOURCE *Publications* • Eugene, Oregon

THE ADDISON COLLECTION

Resource Publications
An Imprint of Wipf and Stock Publishers
199 W. 8th Ave., Suite 3
Eugene, OR 97401

www.wipfandstock.com

PAPERBACK ISBN: 978-1-5326-8812-6
HARDCOVER ISBN: 978-1-5326-8813-3
EBOOK ISBN: 978-1-5326-8814-0

Manufactured in the U.S.A.   08/30/19

Dedication

Frederick A. & Lena T. Newton

FRED AND LENA NEWTON created a loving home life for their children, Figgy, Dele, Sally, and me. Our parents didn't have the opportunities available to them which they provided for us. Dad was raised basically by his grandparents; and at the age of fourteen Mom lost her mother and had already lost two younger sisters.

Dad loved to hunt and fish. There are countless days when he and I would sit along the river bank fishing for rock bass, suckers, and bullheads. He always was able to untangle my fishing line, something I could never do. Since the age of eight, I followed Dad through the woods hunting rabbits on the hill behind the house.

Mom loved her children dearly and was fiercely protective of us. She enjoyed doing crossword puzzles and reading home improvement and garden magazines. Occasionally, Mom would find wild leeks and dandelion greens and take them home to cook, something no one else in the family wanted to eat. What we did like however were her spaghetti dinners that were made using her own tomato sauce recipe. These dinners became a family tradition every Saturday afternoon.

Mom and Dad were totally supportive of everything we did. They worked very hard to give their children a good life. They sacrificed their whole life and suffered the worst of all hurts when my older brother Figgy drowned at the age of eleven, while saving another boy's life. Our family was never the same for the heartache never stopped. However, we remained intact with love and support for each other from that day on.

The Addison Collection is dedicated to my parents to whom I owe everything, my life and my heart.

Contents

Preface

"To me, writing is of prime importance and if I didn't write I would consider it a tremendous failure. To live without recording how I feel, or what I believe, would be to live in vain. I can claim to know very little unless I write it down. It is through the pen that I can best provide homage to my God, service to my country, and justice to myself."

John W. Newton

April 5, 1964

Acknowledgements

Figgy, Dele, & Sally

MY BROTHER, FREDERICK, HAS been my inspiration my entire life. He was a very popular boy, well-liked by classmates and highly respectful of adults. Figgy was president of his 5th grade class, a member of the Boy Scouts, and bat boy for the village men's baseball team.

He was confident and dedicated. As his younger brother I always looked up to Figgy and wished I could be more like him. As with my family, I miss him terribly and so regretful his life was cut so short.

My two sisters, Adele and Sally, have been at the center of my life while growing up. Dele is three years older than me and Sally was seven years younger. I used to go to the movies with Dele and I'd take Sally when she was a very young girl. We had fun together playing board games like Sorry, Parcheesi, and Monopoly. We played rummy and canasta, and put puzzles together on the card table. We'd play table tennis on the extended kitchen table.

Adele moved to Rochester, N.Y. after she graduated from high school, eventually got married and started her own family. A few years later she encouraged me to come to Rochester and find a permanent job. I followed her advice and thus began the second and longest chapter of my life.

Sally remained in our hometown of Addison, N.Y. She had her own family, but her life was highly interwoven with our parents. She looked after them and became a nurse after Dad passed away. From then on, Sally saw Mom on almost a daily basis.

I love Figgy, Dele, and Sally deeply and we'll always be together as brothers and sisters.

Introduction

THE ADDISON COLLECTION WAS written when I was between sev-
enteen and twenty-one years old while living in my hometown of
Addison, New York.

Addison is a small, residential village situated along the Can-
isteo River not far from the Pennsylvania border. Like many towns
in the southern tier, it consists of hills and forests on the north, a
narrow, flat stretch of land that has a highway and railroad tracks
running from east to west. Then there's the river with houses and
businesses on either side. Main Street crosses the river from the
north and extends southward through the center of town.

Main Street is lined with the typical storefronts, and the high
school is located just a block away. In the early 1960s, the town
contained seven grocery stores, six churches, five gas stations, four
bars, three clothing stores, two ice cream shops, and a 195 seat
movie theater. Also, there were a couple of appliance and hard-
ware stores as well as a furniture store, shoe store, news store, and
liquor store. Additionally, there were a coffee shop, barber shop,
pool hall, five-and-dime, and a local newspaper business. At the
5-street intersection on the south end of Main Street were a public
library and a four story town hall which housed the two volunteer
fire departments.

Nearly a third of the homes are located north of the river,
with the rest being distributed across a wider area south of the
business district. Beyond the village are fields and more hills and
forests. The population of Addison in 1960 was approximately
2200 people.

The Addison Collection contains thoughts and sayings, observations, short stories, and a treatise on the United States. The short story, *Space Visitors*, and parts of the treatise, *Our Model Nation*, have been updated since *The Addison Collection* was first written. *It's a Buck* is a true story.

I hope the reader finds this collection interesting, enjoyable, and thought provoking.

John W. Newton

Author's Note:

In addition to this book, the fundamental principles and beliefs in my philosophical works on the nature of reality, the meaning to life, and the value of the human experience were written between 1960 and 1964. This refers to my book series *A Pen Named Man: Our Purpose*, *A Pen named Man: Our Essence*, and *A Pen Named Man: Our Destiny*. The series defines our purpose in life. It further identifies our role to be God's representative on Earth and serve as the gardener and governor of Nature.

Also, the initial chapters of my novel, *Wilderness Nation*, were written during this time. This book offers a unique philosophy of life that's championed by an enlightened Indian tribe of the 1800s. It tells the story of a young man and his Lakota wife's challenge to unify the Native American's and white man's cultures at their trading post in a remote northwest region of the Louisiana Territory.

Thoughts & Sayings

Many people don't realize how close to the ground they are until they bend over to tie their shoe. Indeed, kids have more appreciation of our home, the earth, as they experience contact with it on a regular basis. Children chase after each other and fall and scrape their elbows and knees. They sit on the grass and they play in the dirt. They slide downhill on a sled in the wintertime and a cardboard box in the summer. The grass, dirt, and mud puddles are a part of their everyday life.

A wise spider spins his web to a lamppost. The lamppost provides warmth and light for the spider's comfort. Further, the lamppost attracts moths and other insects that become blinded as they flutter to the bright light. Unknowingly, they fly into the web of the spider and thus become his source of food.

Look after oneself. One might better look more after oneself rather than try to please others, or gain their acceptance by responding in a way you'd think wins their approval. For it is the joke teller who suffers when others criticize him for entertaining them by playing the role of a clown; it is the hard-working entrepreneur who suffers when others belittle him for his business failures; and it is the enabling friend who suffers when others unfairly use him in order to gain their own ends.

Assume responsibility for your own well-being. Everyone must remain vigilant in maintaining good health and seek appropriate medical attention when needed, for it's the gravely ill person who leaves the only known world when he or she gets sick and dies.

Glad I'm older than you. If a young man should say to an old man, "I am glad I am young and not old like you, for I am strong and have many happy years ahead whereas you are weak and can only look forward to death." Let the old man say, " I am glad I am old and near death and you are young, for if we both are to have life everlasting and I die in 1963 and you die in 2023, I will always have been in heaven sixty years longer than you."

What a waste of time is time. We're all given a certain amount of time to live. Unfortunately, we spend much of it by not applying ourselves to accomplish the goals that are waiting for us. Instead, we spend a lot of our time in the pursuit of meaningless and non-productive activities.

The fact that one must die someday seems to make life worth living. If we were granted everlasting life on Earth, it's likely we wouldn't value it as much as we should. Today, we're motivated to appreciate the beauty and wonderment of this life because we know we won't always be here to enjoy it.

Should it be asked if a person lusts for life, let it be said a person lusts for nothing he already has. Typically, we're complacent about the situation we find ourselves in. Quite naturally, we have little or no desire to seek out something we already possess.

I run to death and death runs twice as fast to me. Given how quickly times goes by, it appears that death is coming our way at an accelerated pace. It certainly seems that way the older we get.

It's a Buck

It's Saturday November 26, 1960, a fairly nice day. It's not too cold, just overcast with some sunshine. I'm at home on West Front Street in Addison, N.Y and I've been hunting this morning with Dad up around the Cranberry Pond area.

It's five after two so I think I'll go up back for a while. Let's see, ten shells ought to be enough. Actually I probably won't need any and if I can't get a deer with ten I don't want him. Well I'm all ready to go. All I need is to put on my coat, grab the shotgun, and take off. Oh, I think I'll take an apple along; it'll give me something to munch on if I get hungry. I know darn well those dogs are going to bark when they see me heading up the hillside.

"Quiet Jack, Keep quiet Ringo." Listen to them bark. "You fellows can't go with me this time. I'm going after deer, but maybe we'll go after rabbits tomorrow. It's Sunday and we can hunt them then." It's funny how human-like those two act. You come out all dressed in hunting clothes with boots on and they're ready to go. They don't even have to see the gun. They break their necks to get loose and it's a wonder they don't choke themselves. When you finally unfasten the chain, they take off. They would knock anyone over standing in their way. First they chase around in circles for about five minutes before they settle down and are ready to go hunting. You can see it breaks their hearts, but there is nothing I can do. I'll just start up the hill and let them bark.

It's two-thirty now. It will take me about half an hour to get where I want to hunt and that will leave me about two hours of actual hunting time. Boy, this hill is steep! And the sun is awfully hot. I wish I hadn't worn this heavy coat. Look it! There goes a rabbit!

He was sitting under that little pine tree. If Jack and Ringo were here now they would be long gone over the hill. Well the hardest part of this hike is over now. Sometimes I think you have to be part mountain goat to get up this bank. It's either straight up or straight down depending on where you are standing. I'll rest here for a while and catch my breath. I hope there aren't any hunters up here. I'd hate to be traipsing through the woods and have some city fellow take me for a deer. Well I can't stay here all day—the deer are waiting. Once I cross this field I'll be in the woods where I want to hunt. Boy, this is a beautiful view. I can see all of Addison below me. Cars are on the highway, and across the river beyond Main Street is the school. The river winds down the valley and the church steeples rise above the tree tops. Well, I got to get going.

It's five after three and I finally reached the place where I want to hunt. I'll stand by the television cable that goes down into town. If I do see a deer I hope I don't shoot the cable in two. Then I would be in trouble. From this point I can see throughout the entire woods below. I don't think anything will come from that open field behind me.

That noise! Something's coming! Oh, it's another hunter.

"*Hello, have you seen anything yet?*"

"No, I just got here."

"*Well, I'm going to walk around to the other side of the hill. If I see a buck, I'll send it over.*"

"Yeah, thanks."

That's a good one. If he sees a buck he'll send it over. I've been coming up on this hill for an hour or so every afternoon after school. On Wednesday, I was down on the other side of the hill when that deer snorted and kicked like a horse. I never saw its head to tell whether it was a buck or a doe. From the way it carried on, it must have been a buck. But I couldn't take a chance without knowing for sure. I don't have two hundred and fifty dollars to pay for killing a doe. On Thursday when I came down from this side of the hill, I chased out a couple of deer, but it was too dark to distinguish them. I figured this would be a good place for deer today.

Bang! Bang! Bang! Somebody is shooting at deer across town over on that hill. I hope they don't get him. I can't figure out why everybody always seems to be shooting, and yet for two years I haven't even been able to see one buck.

The sun is beginning to set. No wonder, it's ten after four. The shadows of the trees and bushes are covering the ground. One side of the tree is brightly reflecting the sunlight while the other side is dark and cold. The wind has begun to come up and it is getting chilly. Now I'm glad I wore this heavy coat. Sometimes I wonder what I'm doing here. You get all tired out climbing up and down hills. My legs aching from standing so long in one spot and I'll probably catch cold before I get home. I might better be home where it's warm, reading a book or watching television. Hunting sure can be a waste of time. It wouldn't be so bad if I had a radio to listen to. No, you couldn't still hunt very well with a radio blaring away. I can see down the valley towards Corning. Corning is the place where my dad works at the Glass Works and where I plan to go to college next year.

"Brr . . . " It's getting cold. Twenty after four. I'll leave for home at twenty-five of. Then I'll be home before five while it's still light. It will be great to get these heavy boots off and relax in the chair in front of the TV with a nice cup of hot coffee. I can hear a squirrel chattering somewhere down in the forest. I can hear him, but I can't see him. He seems to be getting closer. There he is. Running up and down the tree trunks, across the limbs. Now he's picking up some hickory nuts in his mouth. There's an old dead tree he is heading towards. I bet that is where he . . . What's that! It's a buck! It's a buck! Raise the gun and fire . . . Bang! I missed. The gun jammed. Charging right at me. The gun's jammed. Turning and going back into the thicket. He's trashing around down there. I'll stand still and take another shot at him when he comes out. It's quiet. He ran off in the other direction. I missed him. Why did I hesitate? Why didn't I chase after him?

It's time to go home. I'll walk over and see where I shot, to see if there's any blood. Not a trace. There's no blood. But what's that down there. It's him. "God, I got him! God, I got him!" He's still.

I gotta get down there. Eight points. One shot through the right shoulder. Set the gun against that small tree. I have to slit his throat and cut his insides out. How warm it feels. This is a messy job but it's worth it. Put the rope around his neck and start pulling.

It's quarter to five. I've got to get home. My knife. Did I leave it behind? No. Ha. I was so excited and yet I didn't leave my knife. He's a nice deer. A good size one too. I got to get home. He was only fifty feet away. He knew I was there, but didn't know where. That's why he didn't run. Just standing there trying to find me out. All I could see was his head, the antlers glimmering with the sunset, just the top of his back. I shot through the brush; not seeing his side but sensing where his heart was located. He reared and charged. Surely I must have missed him. Yet I couldn't. He ran downhill. Any deer badly hit runs downhill. And to think I was so interested in watching the squirrel that I almost missed seeing him entirely.

I reached the field. It's a little after five. He seems heavier than I thought for surely he weighs two hundred pounds. I'm glad it's all downhill. What will my mother say? They will be happy. Should we call my sister in Rochester and tell her. And my grandfather thought hunting was foolish. I will show him how great a hunter I am. I'll rest every few yards. It's getting colder and the deer is heavy. If I put my gun a few feet ahead I can drag him better by pulling with both hands on his antlers. There, this makes it a little easier. Not far to go now. It's dark and the deer is heavy. I can see the light from our house through the trees. The dogs are barking and this time it's probably for food.

It's five-twenty. "*Johnny, Johnny.*" It's Mom, she's calling me. Drop the rope so she doesn't see the deer's head.

"Yes, I'm up here. I'll be down in a few minutes."

"*Did you see anything*"?

"No, nothing."

She asked if I saw anything because she really wants to know if I'm o.k. It's dark and I'm later than normal. It's her way of asking if I'm alright, without coming out and saying it. She went back into the house.

Well, I'll keep dragging the deer down to the house. Listen to those dogs bark. They have to know that I've got a deer. Why else would they be making such a fuss? Whew, I finally reached the house. I'm exhausted! It's twenty minutes to six. It took just over a half-hour to get to where I wanted to hunt, but nearly an hour to drag the deer home. Glad it was all downhill.

Leave the deer just outside the living room window and go into the house.

"*How was it up there? Did you see any deer?*" Dad's asking me.

"Nope, not a thing."

Put the gun down and go get a flashlight from the closet. Now, go over to Grampa.

"Grampa, come over to the window. Look outside. I'm going out there for a minute."

Shine the light on the deer. Look at them! They're all excited! Look how happy they are, including Grampa. I got my first deer!

Retreats of Stones and Mosses

THE TIME IS EARLY morning, the place is North Branch Glendening Creek outside of Addison, New York, and the year is 1958. Several long golden rays of light shoot across the low sky as the sun begins peeking over the hill. The two day rain had changed from a constant downpour to a regular drizzle. It is now a dense mist as the sun seems to chase the straggling clouds out of the sky. The grasses in the field no longer resist the downward pressure of falling rain; rather they are twisted and swept to the ground awaiting the intense warmth of an early summer sun. The hemlock, elm, and pine trees in the nearby forest have soaked up more than their share of water. The last drops of the storm are now dripping from their leaves and splashing upon the scattered dead limbs that have yielded to the heaviest downpour. Sheltered in the deepest thicket are the doe and her fawn, both soaked and shivering. In their large brown eyes can be seen the enduring patience that is learned by all creatures of Nature. Squirrels are busily running up and down the wet tree trunks discovering which limbs the storm has brought down. The field mouse, that literally has been flooded from its borough, scurries about spreading twigs and bits of grasses on stones to dry out for a new nest.

Dividing the field and the forest is a winding brook. The storm has transformed the usually mellow stream into a violent, raging creek. As the woodland creatures come forth into the awaiting sunlight, so emerge the inhabitants of the creek from their retreats of stones and mosses. Minnows are everywhere dashing to and fro braving a fast moving current. They inhabit the entire stream and nearly every pool regardless of its size contains a community of these tiny fish. Life for these minnows can hardly be described as uneventful for the creek itself takes on a multitude of environmental conditions. In the warmest days of summer the stream shallows to such an extent that life is possible only in the larger pools. The creek's bed dries up thus eliminating any passageway by which the minnows can swim from one pool to another. Autumn, with its gusty winds and mild temperatures, brings about a new aspect of life to the stream's inhabitants. For such dwellers as the turtle and crayfish it means digging into the deepest portions of the sandy bed to find an efficient shelter from the approaching winter. To the minnows, autumn means a barrage of infiltrating substances. Multicolored leaves from the adjacent forest are swept so intense into the stream that on many days the entire surface is blanketed with this confetti of the trees. In winter the stream becomes covered with the much more adamant blanket of ice. Those minnows who fail to reach such sanctions offered by the deeper pools eventually become frozen into the ice mass. Spring, the season from which these erratic inhabitants have recently emerged, promises an extensive alteration to the stream's terrain. Adding the scattered cloudbursts to the melting winter snows result in an increase in the speed and volume of flowing water. The turbulent current heaves up the creek's bottom and brings about numerous changes to its format. Disregarding the climatic alterations that accompany each new season of the year, the minnows are subjected to numerous other hazards within their environment. There are always rapids to be scaled, undercurrents to combat, and eddies to avoid.

The brook is open for any minnow to swim upstream and discover the source of his livelihood, or to swim downstream and discover the end of its journey, seemingly a very wide and large river. The minnows would never envision it ending up as the ocean. Throughout the stream's history many of its inhabitants have ventured to discover both the source and end of this fascinating environment. For the minnows the stream runs in only one direction, such as how time runs for man. Of those who seek to discover the source of their stream they are permitted to explore only so far, for they are prevented from discovering the beginning of the creek at points where the water is too shallow to permit life to survive or where waterfalls are so steep that access to the next pool is impossible. Of those minnows that follow the stream to its destination, many are killed and those who aren't never return. As the stream widens into a creek and the creek in turn into a river the dangers periling the minnow's life increase. There are countless larger fish, waterfowl, and other river dwellers awaiting nutrition in the form of a creek minnow. Many of the elder members of the community believe that if it were possible for one of its members to swim from the stream to its end destination unharmed, he would never make it for the distance is too great and the life of a minnow too short. Thus the minnows know partially where their stream begins and know little of the vast sea of life that lies beyond.

The early summer shower has actually increased the hardships of these small fish. An increased speed and force of the water make it difficult for the minnows to swim from one place to another and the muddied water provides covering for their natural enemies.

There is much ado this day for a few of the more adventuresome minnows discover a new link in the stream. The storm has raised the level of the creek and at one point it has overflowed filling a depression four feet deep and nearly fifteen feet long. The passageway from the raging stream to this peaceful bay is very narrow and only twice as deep as a minnow is long. The inlet then widens into a bay nearly five feet broad.

The news is reported and thereupon nearly thirty minnows enter this quiet retreat. The further the school of minnows progress the more awed and excited they become for they find the new lagoon a thriving paradise. Both banks are very steep and covered with a variety of green plants. At the far end of the pond is a wall of stone that houses many shelves and caves the minnows find as excellent homes. The entire floor of the pond is a fine carpet of sand. Surely this is man's Utopia, Adam and Eve's Garden of Eden.

The minnows settle in this new paradise; it's a paradise with abundant food and vegetation, rocky caverns that offer good protection, and an environment that is both calm and mellow. They are as eager and adventuresome as the colonists who ventured to America and established themselves on Roanoke Island in 1587. Some are only curious while others are sincerely grateful that such a place has been found. In the days that follow, the sun grows hotter and the stream loses its raging speed.

It is nearing the end of May and the egg-laying season approaches. The female members of the school are grateful of the pool's calm sandy bottom. Here they can lay their eggs without fear of them being washed away by the swift current. The male members begin taking on their varied dress of scarlet and purple that so vividly distinguish their species every summer. Days are much longer and warmer and consequently the minnows assume a natural tendency of adjusting to environmental conditions. They stay within their cool shelters during the hot days and come out in the night to dash and frolic about. One evening as the minnows venture out from their retreats they find that the passageway to the stream has vanished.

The minnows are quite happy for they no longer need to contend with the forces of a fast moving current or treacherous eddies, nor do they worry about having to scale the steep rapids. Nowhere to be found are their natural enemies. Evidently the dreaded water snake hasn't discovered this pond, for if there was one around no minnow could escape it. The minnow knows he only survives from being eaten by the water snake if the snake bypasses him in favor of a tastier companion. Even the nights are peaceful. This pond's inhabitants have no fear of the swooping claw of the mother raccoon in search of food for her young masked ones.

The minnows' quest for nutrition actually takes the form of a game or sport. When the new pond was created the tiny inhabitants on its banks were as surprised as the minnows that discovered it. Barely a day passes without having ten or twelve insects fall from the banks into the pond. These small insects along with the earthworms either don't realize the pond is there, or else they inadvertently venture too close to the rim and tumble into the water below. The minnows, hour by hour, await the arrival of a tasty insect. The sporting event occurs as the small insect falls from the edge of the bank. Inevitably, every time an insect falls from the bank it brings down several bits of earth and gravel. As the insect hits the surface of the water the awaiting minnows strike. Only one minnow comes up with the insect whereas all the others have a mouthful of dirt. The proud victor dashes off with his meal while the other participants hover ashamedly with a bitter taste in their mouths. Other than similar minor non-pleasantries, the major pressures and problems of ordinary life are gone. This is Utopia. The minnows are inhabitants of perfection and all is theirs.

Young minnows are swimming about everywhere. Not only have the eggs hatched, but they have hatched in a proportion un-recorded in the history of the stream's inhabitants. Normally only about one out of every ten eggs becomes fertilized, and of those fertilized perhaps only three out of every ten grow to adulthood. In this pool most of the eggs were fertilized, and of these nearly all have developed into young minnows. The adult minnows appear overjoyed for never has such a crop of offspring been born to one school of minnows.

Summer continues to progress and day by day the minnows lose part of their pond. The mode of life seems the complete reverse of what it is like in the stream. In the mainstream, the minnows live and die while the stream travels on in its continual state of permanency. Although containing many hazards to the minnow's life, the stream is always moving, always cool, and always nourishing plants and other life. It's the minnow and not the stream that dies. However, these inhabitants feel their environment is dying. The water is stagnant; it has no source, nor does it flow to a greater destiny. The water has become warm and impure with a glossy greenish film over the surface of the pond. The minnows themselves take on the composure of apathy. Their attitude toward life seems as remote as the retreat they occupy. The adult members of the colony relate to the young ones how life is like in the mainstream. They tell of how their friends always hope of living in a paradise such as this. They tell of how the minnows fear the water snake, the raccoon, and other enemies. The young minnows learn of the treacherous current that has formed this haven. The greatest bewilderment to the adult minnows is the zeal and inquisitiveness the young hold in learning about the mainstream. They appear unappreciative of the paradise into which they were born. In fact, they desire a flowing creek as much as their parents desired the paradise they finally found.

The attitude of these young inhabitants is not unpredictable for they know no fear. They've never experienced a turbulent current, nor have they been hunted by a water snake. Additionally, the young minnows show little love and support for others for they cannot distinguish between the emotional extremes of good and bad behavior, or of joy over hardship. They have little actual experience whereby they test their own strengths and desires. On the whole, the new additions to the pool are rather apathetic. The older minnows see the greatest defect of their young in their lack of hope. They have nothing to look forward to, for as far as they know, they were born into having everything they could possibly want. They have no desire for a better life for none could exist. It is quite obvious that the differences between two succeeding generations have never been greater.

One can only wonder if a similar scenario would occur with the human race if a generation of people were able to rediscover the Garden of Eden and thereby become isolated from the trials and tribulations of everyday life.

The unexpected increase in population has brought about a tremendous food shortage. There is no sport in the search for food now. Whenever a minnow finds a bit of food that is too large for one to swallow, it is extracted from his mouth by a group of ravishing companions. The older minnows are more interested in supplying food for the young ones and soon the older ones become weak and exhausted. They couldn't help but wonder if they were better off living in the turbulent, fast-paced creek, rather than in their recently found paradise.

Now, in the hottest days the minnows don't wait until nightfall before they wander about. Neither do they dash about quickly from one place to another. The minnows begin hoping that it will rain. In the creek, rain means the hardships of a fast moving current with muddied water to provide cover for natural enemies, but to the minnows in the pond rain means survival. They remain at the top of the pond in order to get air. Head after head breaks the surface of the water and as a bubble pops at their mouths the minnows disappear into the stale water with a fresh supply of oxygen. The rain never comes and before the day is out four minnows float belly up on the surface of the water. The next day takes half the population, and on the following morning all signs of life are gone.

Two weeks go by and new clouds gather in the western sky. The noon-time sun gradually gets lost in the approaching clouds. The wind picks up and by mid-afternoon sprinkles of rain begin to fall, and by early evening the light rainfall becomes a downpour. Once again, the deer find shelter within the dense thicket while a family of quail huddle together on the lower branches of a nearby pine tree. And other woodland creatures, including squirrels and field mice, are hidden away in the hollows of decaying tree trunks. All are awaiting a let up to the storm.

The rain continues throughout the night. The creek muddies and the water starts to rise. The creek rises to where a trickle of water starts flowing once again into the summer pond. As before, there are a few adventuresome minnows scurrying about and braving the fast moving current. They're out and about eager to explore the latest changes to the creek bed. Soon they discover the newly created entrance to the pond.

The rain lets up, and just before daybreak it stops altogether. More minnows emerge from their hiding places and they too discover the new passageway. Inquisitively, they enter the pond. And so the cycle begins anew.

Space Visitors

THE STORY I HAVE to relate is quite strange, quite frightening, and as far as I know quite true. It occurred a week ago and I haven't been able to remove it from my mind. It is deer season and last Wednesday I was hunting. I was standing at the edge of a steep bank with a huge open field behind me and the forest down below. From where I was standing I could see Reservoir Road, a dirt road that ran alongside the narrow gully which houses the reservoir that supplies the drinking water to the town of Addison, New York. While standing there waiting for a deer to pass by, many things can run through your mind. Part of the time is spent daydreaming, the rest is watching, hoping, and waiting.

I'd been there over two hours when I see this "airplane" in the sky. It was the third plane of the morning and it glistened brightly in the cool sunlight. As it came closer, it appeared much larger than an airplane and made no noise whatsoever. It wasn't a plane at all; it was a spaceship! It came down and landed in the field not two hundred yards away from me. It was a flying saucer just like the ones in comic books and science fiction movies. The only difference was the dome in the center was quite tall, like a long cylinder and rounded at the top. The structure was quite large, being longer than a commercial jet airliner. The saucer was of a silvery, aluminum-type surface, and was blindingly bright as it reflected the sunlight.

The spaceship was actually like the one my family had seen just a few months earlier. My mother came home from working at Westinghouse in Bath, New York, and after walking up the steps from the road, she came into the house very excited. She said to come outside and look up into the sky. It was mid-week about 12:30 a.m. in August, 1961. My father, sister, and I went outside and sure enough there was what appeared to be a flying saucer, as I described, traveling above the center of town. It came from the east and suddenly veered southwestward. You could see the tall cylindrical outline sitting on a saucer-shaped disk. A bright light on the front was flashing every few seconds, and when it flashed, the outline of the saucer became visible. It made absolutely no noise, and in a matter of a couple of minutes, it was gone.

Today, a new spaceship just landed in the field. A door opened downward and three small figures descended a ramp. At this point, I was quite scared. I was too scared to turn and run, and too scared to take my eyes off them. I had a sick feeling in the pit of my stomach and my heart was racing. I stood there shaking as they approached. I shoved the safety off on the gun, but I don't know even if I would have dared to fire at them. You know all your life, you hear fantastic tales of flying saucers and of little green men from Mars who have ray guns that can disintegrate you. You form an impression about such unknown beings, and then when you're confronted by similar characters you act according to your long established impressions. They stood no more than four feet tall and wore sparkling white suits as they approached. The one in the lead raised the greenish-tinted visor over his face and took off his helmet. His skin color was of a pale, light gray. The three looked just like small people, except from what I could tell they had no hair whatever, and had what appeared to be undeveloped ears or no ears at all.

"*Do not be afraid,*" the one in the lead said, "*No harm will be inflicted upon you.*" I said nothing. I just stood there bewildered.

"*We have come from a far off place unknown to you or your kind. Can you speak?*"

"Yes . . . Yes . . . ," I said.

"*Your kind is very strange. We come to your land and you are afraid of us. We are strangers in a strange world and yet it is you, not us, who hold fear.*"

"What do you want? What are you doing here?" is all I could utter.

"Good, you can speak," the tallest of the three said. *"We come to your land only to see, only to observe. We observe your development and we know you humans fight wars every eighteen days, when based on our time frame of reference. Each time the wars are larger and kill more people. Soon you will destroy yourselves."*

"You speak English, and what do you mean wars every eighteen days?"

"Oh, we must explain to you. In this world, you have pets called dogs. It is common belief among your kind that for every year of human life a dog has seven. While an infant of your kind is but three years old, a puppy born at the same time would have gone through what's equivalent to babyhood, childhood, and early adulthood. Similarly, a housefly lives but three weeks. In three weeks' time, a housefly goes through childhood and adulthood in what is but a tiny portion of a person's life. A fly does in three weeks all that a man does in eighty years, and neither one is pressed for time. Also, you have giant Sequoia trees in your forests that live longer than two thousand years. What a man does in eighty years only comprises one twenty-fifth of the tree's life. Your life, from the time you are born until you die, has elapsed and the tree is equivalently not old enough to attend kindergarten.

Your time is equivalent to one five-hundredths of our time. Every one year in our life is equal to five hundred of your years. From the time one of us is born until he dies, over eighteen generations of your people have passed. One day in our year is equal to over sixteen months of your life.

As you wonder why we speak your language, it is simply because we've had a long time to learn. We have studied people with your language and learned from them. If you think our actions and thought processes should be five hundred times slower you are right, relatively speaking. But that only applies to our kind, within our homeland, within our civilization. However, we've had lots of time, and much practice, to adjust our life processes. We're able to make them compatible to many of the types of life below us. And when we explore new worlds, this is what we do. I must say your human civilization is one of the more unique ones that we've encountered. We frequent your planet occasionally but not as often as we do others. Yet, if we choose we will own your world one day."

"Why would you want to own this land? What is here for you?"

"Many times we have come to your planet and taken samples of all types of plant and animal life. We have reproduced the conditions under which they live, and now most of the extinct creatures of your earth are thriving in our land. They are in places for our recreation—like you have zoos for your animals and aquariums for your fish. There are other species we raise and use for food just as you raise cattle and sheep. Such types of life are tasty snacks for our pleasure."

"What do you want with us? Is it for food? For slavery? To put us in your zoos? You may be more intelligent, but if you plan on doing something like that, you're not better or more moral than we."

"That is correct. We are no different than you, just another type of life. Regarding eating other types of life, we do that in order to survive. It's not a question of being more or less moral than you. After all, don't you eat chickens, cows, and pigs in order to live? What are you doing here in this field, right now? Deer hunting? Don't you care about those animals? Don't they have feeling like you? Don't they exhibit thoughts and emotions? You see it when they are protecting their young. Don't they exhibit pain when they are injured?"

"Yes, they do. And yes we care about them. But we do eat meat to survive. We also eat fruits and vegetables. This is how Nature works.

You must also know that if you come after us, we have weapons and we won't surrender without a fight."

"We understand. We are not invulnerable for we too die, and you have weapons that can destroy us. You see we are composed of elements and substances not too different from those found in your world."

"Why are you telling me all of this"?

"It doesn't matter what we tell you for who will believe you? You can tell this to whomever you wish, but will they listen? That's the dilemma you face. However, do not feel alone, for there are many people in your land who have seen our space saucers.

On our last trip to your world, we took a very interesting account of your countrymen's behavior. In a certain region of your nation your people have seen our saucer intermittently over a period of two months. Yet to us these two months are only two hours and fifty-three minutes long. In two hours and fifty-three minutes we fly over a portion of your country and to us this time is rather infinitesimal. But to your people it was a two month period of uncertainty. The people spread various rumors of the size and shape of our ship. Your government sends military personnel to interview the people. Jet aircrafts fly over the area trying to intercept us. If one of your jets follows us for two hour of your time we are only aware of it for less than fourteen and one-half seconds. In this quarter of a minute, we are not too impressed or worried about your aircraft. Those pilots tell others and the others think they are hallucinating. No one of your species believes unless he sees it with his own eyes, and then he'll make excuses to contradict what he sees. Your government will not confirm that your people see our spacecraft; it will say the people see meteorites, conventional aircrafts, blimps, or satellites. How could your government confirm the reports? It would only panic the people into worrying over something they have no control. And you humans will be long gone when the time arrives for us to decide whether we wish to exploit your planet or not.

We can wait indefinitely, for ten years for us is equivalent to 5,000 years for you. Besides, we have other planets and worlds to deal with that are many times larger and more interesting than Earth. You are a strange race, as you humans have goals of slowly, but surely, approaching the perfection of yourselves as well as your environment here on earth. Yet many of your goals and values we find as unimpressive and of little consequence. For instance, we do not share in your quest for perfection. Think of it this way, the universe does not belong to you alone and what you want isn't necessarily what others want."

"We are just here. We are trying to live our lives as best we can. We try to live the way God wants us to live."

"From observing you nation, we know you desire to improve the living conditions for everyone. We also know you hold religious beliefs that bond you to the creator of this universe. You call this creator God, and a major quest in your life is to someday unite with God in everlasting life. Is this correct?"

"Yes, you are correct. Our Judeo-Christian foundation teaches us that our life is temporary here on earth and under the proper condition we can be accepted into the Kingdom of Heaven, where it will be a perfect and eternal existence. To ensure that occurs, Christians believe we must accept the Lord as our savior. We should also live a moral life and not harm other people whom we meet in life. The danger of not accepting the Lord, or of committing evil acts, is to end up in Hell with eternal damnation."

"That's an interesting basis of belief and from our exploration of your planet we know that similar understandings are held by several of your world's major religions. We too have beliefs. We believe in God. We also believe in a life hereafter, but we don't dwell on it. We place less emphasis on the existence of a heaven or hell. Instead, we place more emphasis on the inherent value of this existence.

Let me ask you this. How do you know that either heaven or hell exists?"

"They exist because our fundamental religious books, like the Bible, teach us they do. And we know it because we accept our books' teachings completely. More than just believing, we know for sure that God and heaven exist. We rejoice in knowing one day, when we die, we will be reunited in heaven with God and the people we love."

"And how do you know that heaven is a good place and that hell is bad"?

"Again we know it because that's what our religion teaches us. We are taught that if we live a good life on earth and do good deeds, we'll have the opportunity to go to heaven where we'll be rewarded. Conversely, if we do bad deeds and hurt or murder others, we will be delivered to hell where we'll be punished."

"*Like you, we don't have everlasting life in our world. However, we don't know that heaven exists, or that's it's a good place. Similarly, we don't know that hell is a bad place if it too exists.*"

"What we believe provides us with hope and guidance relative to the way we live our lives."

"*Consider this. Suppose you were born into heaven and never first lived on earth. How would you know that heaven is a good place?*"

"I don't know how a person would know."

"*Answer this. Since you're born on earth and want to get into heaven, does that mean heaven has degrees of rewards which are based upon how deeply you believe in you religion, or how many good deeds you accomplish on earth?*"

"Again, I don't know. I would say that heaven doesn't have degrees of rewards. I would say the reward is universal and equal for all who are accepted to be with the Lord."

"*Then how about hell. If you were born into hell, how would you know that it was bad? And since you are born on earth, does hell have different levels of punishment based upon how strongly you disbelieve in God, or on how many evil acts you commit on earth?*"

"I don't know that either. But I would think that indeed hell punishes those proportionately to how bad they were when alive on earth."

"*You see if you were born into heaven or into hell, you wouldn't know whether it was good or bad.*

That's because, the only thing you'd know about heaven is what was going on there and what was happening to you, and you'd accept it because you wouldn't know that any alternative ever existed. In heaven, there is no range of behavior from good deeds to evil deeds, nor no range of thought and emotion from good to bad. In heaven, everything is uniformly good throughout. The same is true, although it's uniformly evil, for hell."

"I never thought of life that way."

"*Thus, do you now see why we value this life so much? Yes, it isn't perfect. But, for your species of life it has the good components of health, love, compassion, and caring. It also has the bad elements of disease, pain, sin, and hate. But because of these extremes, and everything in between, you can live your life knowing what you want to strive for, knowing what you want to achieve in life, and knowing where you want to end up. You wouldn't have this perspective if you were born initially into heaven; or if you were born first into hell. That is why we find such a deep sense of satisfaction in living in this universe, at this time, and as who we are!"*

"I don't know why heaven is so important to us here on earth. But it is! Everyone would like eternal life that is beautiful, happy, and good. It is in heaven. That's what we desire."

"Why do you think we are more satisfied than your people are with our existence in this universe? Is it because we have the ability to adjust our thinking and actions to coincide with the forms of life we encounter in our travels? Is it because we have such a long life span? Or perhaps, is it because we don't wish to downplay our existence here and we truly appreciate our assigned place in it?"

Well, at that point in time they decided to leave. They boarded their spacecraft and within moments took off. There was no burnt grass or anything else to mark the spot where they had landed. I looked around the field and everything was the same as it was before. The grass was slightly blowing in the wind, the sky was blue, and the sun was bright. I decided to quit hunting and go home. I was bewildered.

All the way home, I thought about this encounter. "Would anybody believe me if I told them? Would they say it was just a dream?"

I couldn't help but think that the visitors from space made some important points. Maybe we spend too much of our time looking for something else, that being a perfect existence either here or in heaven. Perhaps we don't put enough emphasis on the meaning and beauty of life on Earth. If we truly have faith in God and believe we'll go to heaven if we live a moral life, then we shouldn't worry about it so much. Although we ought to strive to make ourselves and our society better, we should also appreciate the value of this life as it is.

I was thinking "Our world was made for us to experience and enjoy as God commands, so we ought to make the most out of what it has to offer. As human beings we should live as God has created us to live."

Authorship

A limited vocabulary doesn't necessarily mean a limited mind; and an elegant vocabulary need not necessarily reflect an elegant mind.

The greatest thought may cross a person's mind in a matter of seconds, but it takes days before it is remembered, weeks before it's written, years before it is read, and centuries before it's followed.

One would do better to carry a pen with him at all times for it is easier to write as you think rather than try to write what you thought.

Sometimes an author may wonder if he's wasting his time by writing. He thinks he might better spend his time reading. But alas, that which he reads has been written by another, and it is this other writer who also wondered if he wasted his time.

If one should ask how many books a person should write, let the person write as many books as his thoughts allow, for surely books are written from thought and an author's thoughts far exceeds his handwriting.

Should an individual decide to use the pen to express his views, feelings, and philosophy of life, then the person should write while he is young, say in his early twenties. At this point, his ideas are original, untarnished, and unbiased. One's penmanship may be rough and unrefined, yet more importantly it will be little affected by the works of others. The author can spend the next ten to twenty years to improve his grammar, style, and penmanship, as well as do research on his own ideas from the major authors of history. The individual can then revise his original writings, with the ease of better style plus the enrichment gained from other writers. Most importantly, the writer's original ideas won't become corrupted by his studies; rather they will become useful.

If an author at the age of twenty has the thoughts of a man of sixty, let us hope that at the age of sixty this man has the thoughts of one of twenty. Although he may be unhappy because he's not interpreting events from the same perspectives as people of his own age, his life nonetheless will not be in want.

It makes little difference at what age an author writes, for a person of twenty in 1960 may unknowingly have the same thoughts and write nearly identical lines as what an author of sixty wrote in 1540.

An author in learning, discovering, or investigating Existence has no sources or reference books he can turn to. However, in doing research for a book on human life an author has as many sources to turn to as the number of people who have lived. And in doing research on the United States, an author has a lesser number of sources to choose from, specifically those people who have lived in America since 1776.

Should an individual be asked why he writes about human beings, the author would say that I write of people and for people because I am a person. Everyone functions as he or she is biologically and psychologically composed to function. The author would say, I was born a man; I am living as a man; and I shall die a man. Should the author be asked if that which he writes may someday be lost in the ruins of history, the author can say that as long as my thoughts have been written down their immortality is both enshrined and assured.

An interesting curiosity that spans from one generation to the next is how people can live and die and not record their beliefs. It seems the justification would be that a person knows what his beliefs and principles are, but fails to write them down because they've already been recorded by someone else, or the person just doesn't want to take the time to do it. But how can we know if an individual holds such knowledge, or a unique perspective on life, unless he records it.

If a writer sincerely impresses someone he or she has written about, it is likely the person he wrote about has impressed the author in some way. A similar observation can be made in the world of art, for how can an artist flatter a beautiful woman on canvass unless he's initially pleased by the sight of her beauty?

If an author says I believe what I write rather than I reason what I write, then anyone attacking the validity of the statement will be attacking the writer's faith rather than his rationale. For if the author already believes what he says, he may be trying to affirm his beliefs to himself or to others through reasoning. And no one can say one's religion is inaccurate, for who can say that a person's religious beliefs are in error. Who can say the faith of the Christian is better than the faith of the Jew, better than the faith of the Buddhist, or better than the faith of anyone else?

What is one's purpose or goal in life? How high on the ladder of success can a person climb? Is there a limit according to the times and conditions of society? Probably the presidency of the United States is the most prestigious office that's available to an American today. But who can say the presidency is more important or yields greater influence than that of the British monarchy of the 1600s, or of the Roman emperors of the 400s BC. The most important position a person can hold changes from generation to generation and from society to society.

And if a person was President of the United States would he be satisfied, or would he rather be the leader of a religion. The individual who yields influence over a society's moral standards and religious beliefs is far more influential than a person who controls a country's government. But who can say that anyone who establishes a major religion of the world is more important than the leader of any other religion such as Abraham, the founder of the Jewish religion, Confucius, the primary teacher of Confucianism, or Buddha, the prophet of Buddhism. Naturally Abraham is more important to the Jewish people, just as Confucius and Buddha are more important to the Confucianists and Buddhists.

As a human being, the leader of a religion may not necessarily be the ultimate position that's attainable. That is, it may not be the political or clerical position that's most important to a person, say to someone such as an author.

Rather, what may be most important to an author is that he's able to write what he wishes, feels, believes, and knows. It may not matter so much if what he says is true or false, useful or useless, important or unimportant, although the author would hope it is true, useful, and important. What might matter more, is that he records it.

Our Model Nation

Life and Country

I HAVE REVIEWED THREE major areas of Life; those being Existence (God), the human race, and one's personal life. I've looked at the significance of each as it pertains to living within a single country, that being the United States of America. Should it be asked in what order should they be ranked, let it be said the order doesn't matter. All are interrelated and significant regarding societal life in America.

Existence is of incomparable majesty. God provides life for all living creatures, and through God's grace every human being born is a benefactor. God grants that each one of us is a unique and special being of his creation and given a world to enjoy with all its beauty every day of our life. Each object of substance and every being of life owes its entire creation and life to Existence. God is the giver, Life is the gift, and Existence is the domain.

Absolutely nothing can exist without God, yet God can exist without anything. Each being, element, substance, material, action, and feeling is a counterpart to Existence and cannot be sustained without Life. Mankind exists because of Life, where Life is the gift of God. Man can reproduce man; but he cannot create the quality of Life. That unique and special quality is already there. Life is fundamental of and previous to the producer and the produced. The make-up of Existence and its interrelationship with God and Life is fully described in *A Pen Named Man: Our Purpose*.

What's the importance of the human species and where does it fit in? All Life is born from Existence. Life is the gift of God and mankind is one of its recipients. The human race represents a species of life that has qualities and capabilities uniquely separate from all other types of life.

There's a special kinship among the people of the world. All people are alike and share the same biological needs and life processes. Similarly, they all share the same mental capabilities of intelligence and thought, as well as the same basic emotions of love and hate, joy and sadness, courage and fear. People the world over seek truth and honesty, and they strive to improve the overall quality of life. They work and play, smile and frown, as living representatives of God. The importance of animate life on Earth, the role of mankind, and the need to synthesize the biological and non-biological components of the human organism into a compatible, workable union are reported in *A Pen Named Man: Our Essence.*

What then is the importance of one's individual life? In the day-to-day living, an individual's life is most important. Everyone has an identical, innate nature to live and survive in the world. One's physical well-being and emotional security, along with the desire for happiness make life worthwhile for each one of us.

Furthermore, we can ask, what's the importance of living in America? What does it mean? This country, i.e. the United States of America, is important because it provides a place and a time where a person can live in a socio-economic system that supports a free and independent way of life. It provides a culture with a heritage that's based on individual rights and liberties.

The government of the United States offers every citizen the opportunity to live and work in a safe environment that's protected by police and military forces. It's an environment where the citizen knows that justice will be served based on fairness via a jurisprudence system of courts, trial by jury, and a utilization of penal institutions. The American system likewise provides the citizen with broad educational opportunities, important health care support, and an assortment of useful social services. Additionally, it allows a person to work in an occupation of one's choosing, along with the ability to live anywhere in the country that he or she wishes.

Of the human race, the United States of America, and one's personal life it is difficult to rank their order because they're all interrelated. It's not unreasonable for a person to have difficulty deciding the most important from among his fellow man, his country, or his personal quest for happiness.

In everyday life where no crisis is involved, it's fairly certain that one's personal welfare is of most importance. Everyone goes about his or her daily routine at work or play and tries to make the day as productive and pleasant as possible.

However, when unexpected dangers arise, human behavior is less predictable and an individual may put the welfare of others above his own. For example, consider the individual who takes risks to help strangers such as rescuing someone out of a burning car, or jumping into a fast moving river to save another person from drowning. And what about the fireman who runs into a burning building to lead a trapped family out to safety; or a police officer who physically tackles a desperate criminal who is armed with a hand gun. Further, consider the soldier who pledges his life to protect the country by serving in the military and is ready to engage the enemy when so ordered. These are cases where people are called upon to make decisions that jeopardize their own lives for the benefit of others.

Of all the governments in the world, the government of the United States is one of the most accomplished. Especially in America, it's difficult to separate the commitment to one's fellow man with the interests for personal success, for in one respect the United States is founded on the basic principles of an individual's right to life, freedom, and the pursuit of happiness. In a broader respect, it's founded on the formation of a more perfect union that's designed to secure domestic tranquility and promote the general welfare of all of its citizens. Collectively, these approaches to social justice and equality can be summarized as humanitarianism. The two inseparable areas of dedication, for oneself and humanity, are united and promoted in this country called America.

Of Existence, the human species, an individual's life, and the realm of government, government is the only entity that's created by human beings. Government is established for people and administered by them. Without question, government is an extremely important social institution. The role of government is to ensure the safety of all citizens and establish a system that provides equality and justice for all human interactions. Along with the social institutions of family, religion, education, employment, etc., the importance of the institution of government is described in *A Pen Named Man: Our Destiny*.

Any worthwhile attempt to gauge the relative importance of Life's key entities ought to consider the degree of control people have over the area in question. An individual person has greatest control over his own life and the daily activities he participates in. In America an individual citizen has, by way of his vote, limited control over the government of his country. And as far as the species of man is concerned, an individual has very little control. In actuality, relative to free will and behavior, he has control of only one member which is himself. For the most significant sector we've discussed, Existence or God, the individual has no control.

Finally, another means of putting the major facets of Life into proper perspective is to use a measure we're highly familiar with, which is the emotion of love. For instance, look at the love we hold for specific people in our lives. We might ask, can a man categorically rate the degree of love and importance he holds for his wife, his mother, his daughter, and his sister? An honest person would say the love he holds for his wife, mother, daughter, and sister, are basically the same. He may love his wife for one set of reasons and love his mother for another set of reasons, but there are certain reasons which are the same for loving all, his wife, mother, daughter, and sister. Similarly, a man has certain reasons for loving God and humanity, other reasons for loving his country, and still different reasons for loving his personal successes. Yet among all of these, there are basic commitments which are common to each. For sure, he is dedicated to God and to mankind for some of the same reasons he's dedicated to his country and his own ambitions.

Our Model Nation

Mankind at the Crossroads

IT APPEARS THAT THE human race is always at a crossroad. Certainly it is now! Mankind is in the early stages of a new and challenging adventure, and over the past few decades it has begun to embark on a new journey involving the exploration of outer space. The universe is the last and largest frontier. It's a vast frontier for us to traverse and space exploration represents the natural continuation of our manifest destiny.

A major challenge of the people of the world is to draw together; that is, to establish and work towards common social and cultural goals. To achieve those goals, we must remove the barriers of distrust, disrespect, and ill-will from governmental, religious, and socio-economic systems across the world.

Indeed, the people of the world are drawing closer together. Modern communication and transportation networks provide people the world over with an opportunity to conveniently interact and intermingle with one another. Likewise, the development of world-wide economic networks, which involve the manufacture and sale of consumer products, and the delivery of broad-based social services promote a dependency among the numerous nations of the world.

Space exploration too can be a catalyst that encourages the several nations of the world to work together as they explore this last frontier. Adversaries from outer space, unforeseen life-threatening dangers, and new diseases which we may encounter during space flight, would likely force the people of the world to come together.

Mankind should attempt to put his house in order before he sets out to investigate outer space however. Ideally, mankind ought to eliminate the shortcomings of his political, economic, and social institutions on Earth before he attempts to colonize other planets.

Before we travel to other celestial bodies, we ought to improve our society on Earth. Before we begin to erect additional societies in other worlds, we must develop our society to its greater potential. Thus, we'll have a more perfect model to duplicate elsewhere. We must strengthen our social structure. We must eliminate the current problems of substance abuse, corruption, and crime. We must eliminate poverty and hunger. We must put an end to injustice in the world. We must dedicate ourselves to the moral and righteous causes of man. We must promote and preserve the major institutions of mankind that are important to us. A solid house is built on a strong foundation. So too, new societies are stronger when established from a sound model.

God isn't favorable to one society over another. A nation which more closely follows fair and just principles is the nation that ultimately prevails. To assure the preservation of its social structure, the people must strive to improve morally and ethically. Because a nation is powerful, doesn't mean that it is right. When a nation is right, it is great with no misgivings involved. At that point, the nation is following the wishes of God.

Similarly, because you are alive doesn't mean that you're right. Today, a nation may feel it has the most gifted people on Earth simply because they represent the living generation. These people may have extreme faith in their God. They may preside over highly advanced socio-economic and political systems. However, looking back in history, nation after nation thought this way. Irrespectively, they made mistake after mistake.

It appears that every few generations or so, society has to reshuffle its priorities. It has to redirect itself and dedicate its people to a higher, more worthy cause. This was the case with the United States of America. In the 1640s, the nation was starting out as a new social structure. A modern society was beginning to form.

The early immigrants dedicated themselves to carving out an empire from an untamed wilderness. Then, over 100 years later the inhabitants took on a new challenge. In the 1770s the American people dedicated themselves to the erection of a free, independent society with a fair, representative government. Nearly 100 years later, another crisis reached an explosive stage. The rights and freedom of all people were tested by a civil war. In the 1860s the people once again rededicated themselves to the equality of man and the preservation of the union.

Now Americans and the world are taking on their biggest challenge relative to their dedication to a greater cause. They are embarking on the exploration of outer space. As of now, we are still in the pre-exploration days. We have not yet reached the days of Cortez, Balboa, or Ponce de Leone. America was discovered by Columbus in 1492. In 1776 it was proclaimed a free and independent nation, dedicated to the principles that all men are created equal and endowed by their creator with certain unalienable rights. It took 284 years for this new founded land of freedom and opportunity to be tamed and cultivated. It took 284 years to develop a society of people who had the determination to succeed and the ingenuity to progress. It took 284 years to establish a land where the government offered guaranteed liberty and an opportunity to pursue individual happiness.

In 1969 a new generation of American explorers landed on the moon. However, the human race has not yet reached the 1492 of space adventure. When we do, we'll go forward. Our manifest destiny will be revived as the last and largest frontier is penetrated.

Our Model Nation

Melting Pot of the World

AMERICANS COMPRISE A VERY fortunate society of people and are in a position to contribute significantly to major advances in social living. By the natural progression of the culture of the human species, the American society is in a position to pioneer advances across the major universal institutions of mankind. The American people are at the forefront of social progress in many respects as they face problems and undergo growing pains that are likely to be the problems and growing pains of the entire world. America experiences and solves many important problems that someday will likely be experienced and solved by the entire world.

To cite an example, consider the integration of the African-American into American culture. Following many decades of cruel slavery, unfair treatment, and discrimination, the African-American was able to gain equal status with his fellow citizens and achieve the opportunity for life, liberty, and the pursuit of happiness. In the centuries ahead, the entire world will experience a desegregation of all the races and sub-races of mankind. We are at the beginning of global integration among the people of the world. In the decades ahead, major ethnic groups, nationalities, and races will want to integrate into an overall world society.

America has been called the melting pot of the world. Indeed, it's the melting pot of a variety of communities of people. A significant number of immigrants of many nationalities, ethnic groups, and religious sects came to America during the late 1800s and early 1900s. They came to America to settle and seek out a better life. Over the years they intermingled and intermarried, and a more homogeneous society of people developed. This became the twenty-first century American. Someday the entire world will intermingle and intermarry. A new world society of people will develop. The multi-lineage individual of America today more closely represents the multi-lineage person of the world tomorrow. The typical American of today most closely represents what the typical citizen of the world will be like in the future.

The average American of today is pragmatic in character. He is fairly materialistic relative to possessions and other amenities in life which include a home, automobile, furniture, clothing, going out to dinner, taking vacations, etc. He is judgmental of behavior and attitude. At times, he can be hypocritical and employ a double standard when judging his own behavior vs. the behavior of others.

The typical American has a strong moral outlook on life. He has a solid set of values centered on respect and fairness, freedom and opportunity, equality and justice. He strongly rejects groups that teach violence as the means to achieve a goal. Through dedication and hard work, an American believes personal achievement is both desirable and measurable relative to attaining occupational success. The American tends to evaluate nearly every situation in a moral context. That is, issues of life are looked upon as right or wrong, good or bad. Additionally, he's frequently for the underdog in sports and other competitions.

There is a substantial degree of freedom guaranteed to the individual living under the American design of government. America's democratic form of government is characterized by the legislative, executive, and judicial branches, each of which has specific duties to perform. Governmental officials are elected by and representative of the public as a whole. An individual can have freedom of thought with limited influence imposed on him from the state. He has freedom to choose his own political principles as well as his own religion. Likewise, a person has freedom to choose one's philosophy of life, which includes his set of values, convictions, and social outlook. Thereby, a person has the freedom to pursue one's intellectual as well as emotional happiness. These are the freedoms of the mind.

The individual is also guaranteed several freedoms of behavior. This includes the freedom of speech. It includes the freedom to obtain an education and the freedom to work in an occupation of one's choosing. It also includes the freedom to own property, buy and sell products, interact with one's fellow man, and pursue leisure time activities. These freedoms are generally subjected to the social norms of the time.

The political and social-economic system of the future will reflect the principles of opportunity and fairness for the average citizen. It will reflect principles based on the rights of the common man and the protections he's afforded in society. It will also take note of the responsibilities each citizen has to support and maintain the state.

From a practical point of view, it's wise to develop a universal model for the advancement of social living. And an excellent place for that to occur is in the United States of America. The American economic system of free enterprise has been successful to the extent that people only have to work about one-third of their waking hours to sustain themselves. By working forty hours per week, they're able to provide the necessities of life and various material comforts they need. Because they don't have to work the entire day to meet their basic needs, American citizens have the time to think about and pursue humanitarian goals. Someday, all major regions of the world will have the resources and time to work toward the beneficial goals of universal education, universal health care, and a universal socio-economic employment structure.

Our Model Nation

Balance Natural Government with Institutional Government

ONE WAY TO DESCRIBE the history of the United States government is to say it represents the gradual maturation of an institutionalized government as it approaches and embraces the natural government of mankind. The process is aptly illustrated by the chronological development of the U.S. constitution.

The question arises as whether the institutional government of America should remain confined and separate from natural government, or should it become entirely engrossed in it? A persistent approach of many throughout the world is to incorporate natural law into the constitutions of institutionalized governments. This takes the form of edicts in social justice, civil right laws, and entitlements legislation.

The institutional government of America includes the U.S. constitution and state constitutions as well as laws passed by congress and state legislatures. It also includes constitutional amendments, court rulings, and edicts derived from common law. The Declaration of Independence of the United States actually introduces the interrelationship between natural law and institutionalized government when it states " . . . and to assume among the powers of the earth, the separate and equal station to which the Laws of Nature and of Nature's God entitle them . . . "

The U.S. federal government can provide a place, these United States, and purchase a time, from 1776 on, through which each member of society can exercise his or her natural government. Indeed, the natural government is a personal government and is guaranteed to every citizen of the United States. The institution-alized government, on the other hand, is the government of all, i.e., the public. Institutionalized government operates in matters of general concern, whereas natural government is concerned with individual liberties. Basically natural government represents the singular spokes of a wheel, whereas institutional government stands for the entire wheel itself.

Natural government is highly focused on each of us taking charge of our behavior and seeking out what we desire in life as long as we don't obtain it at the expense of others. Rather, we achieve our goals in life through honest, hard work with concern for our fellow man. We accept others as equals and follow the rules of fair play, whereby we don't harm others in either emotional or physical ways.

Institutional government, on the other hand, focuses on the public good and attempts to monitor citizen behavior so everyone receives just treatment under the law. Its goal is to prevent personal injury or harm. To that extent institutional government establishes a police force, legal system, set of courts, and penal system to ap-prehend, try, judge, and then dole out punishment to anyone who harms or unjustly takes advantage of others.

What institutional government does for natural government is to ensure that natural government remains in place for all the citizens. It guarantees that natural government remains uniform and is applied equally. It doesn't allow a person to exercise natu-ral government according to one's desires, where an individual may feel it's perfectly all right to steal another's property, harm another person, or even to take another person's life. Rather, in-stitutional government establishes the parameters by which the citizens are able to exercise their desires and wishes in a secure social environment.

Throughout history, people have learned there are numerous benefits to living in a society rather than living alone in Nature. Social living provides broader opportunities for people relative to employment, housing, clothing, and food procurement. Fur-ther, there are advantages in all other major areas of life including communication, transportation, educational, health care, and recreation. To secure these benefits, the people have a duty to obey the laws in place and they have a responsibility to support government through whatever requirements are necessary such as adhering to moral standards, paying taxes, or serving in the military.

The role of institutional government relative to natural government then is to put the natural government of its citizens on an equal keel, characterized by the fair and just treatment of everyone. In the sense that benefits are afforded and responsibilities are met, the value of institutional government is to ensure the natural government of mankind is executed on a fair platform.

Natural government has been long known to mankind, for natural government is the first activity of social conduct across the human race Natural government came into existence with the birth of the human race and will last throughout its lifetime. Throughout history, parents have taught their children the principles of natural government. They have done so through involvement in family, church, and social events.

Everyone knows the value of right over wrong, knowledge over ignorance, and truth over falsity. Likewise, everyone recognizes the importance of freedom over slavery and justice over injustice. We understand the value of honor over guilt as well as pride over shame. Furthermore, we all understand the value of love over hatred. These have been taught and learned, seen and experienced, and promoted in many ways throughout human history.

How does an individual execute his or her natural government? What the person has to do is decide what is right. One must always do what is right. It's not difficult in deciding between right and wrong, and the execution of what's decided isn't difficult either. And who among us is to accept the responsibility for deciding what the truth is? Who decides what is right? It's the individual, every one of us, who decides what is the right thing to do, without causing harm to others.

Thus, it's time for each person to behave as a mature member of the human race. We must do this in order to justify the existence of our species.

Everyone must justify his or her existence. You are a human being, nothing more and nothing less. You must live as you're biologically composed to live, and live as you're psychologically supposed to. If you are unsure about this, then ask God. If you find it difficult to distinguish between right and wrong, all you have to do is pray to God and he'll respond faster than you will know.

Natural government then is derived from an independent people living in a free society such as the United States of America. And who protects the American democracy? It is the institutional government of the United States. The American government should have no critics, in this respect, for it protects the citizens and guarantees them a place to practice their natural government. And natural government is always more encompassing than institutionalized government.

The institutionalized government of the United States will not overshadow nor dominate the application of natural law by its citizens. As we said, it will reserve a section of the planet where natural law can be practiced by free and independent people who benefit from its use for an indefinite period of time.

Our Model Nation

Where Natural Law Conflicts with Institutional Law

AN EXAMPLE OF INSTITUTIONAL law conflicting with natural law is illustrated by the passage and subsequent repeal of the eighteenth amendment to the U.S. constitution. The eighteenth and twenty-first amendments represent the case of a moral opinion subjected to the jurisdiction of institutional government. The eighteenth amendment prohibited the manufacture, sale, or transportation of intoxicating liquors within the territorial jurisdiction of the United States.

The eighteenth amendment was repealed by the twenty-first amendment, which demonstrated that the federal government could not assume the responsibility for deciding the consumption of intoxicating liquor was immoral and against the natural law of mankind. It's the individual's decision on whether or not to make, transport, and sell alcohol. Likewise, it is the individual's decision on whether or not to buy and consume alcohol. This represents an opinion that lies within the jurisdiction of natural government.

Generations from now, people will look back on our country and wonder how the people could enact a law and then make that law null and void fourteen years later. Why would a country nullify a law which appeared to reflect American morality at the time? Well, the eighteenth amendment was passed by a two-thirds vote of congress and approved by three-fourth of the states' legislatures because there was sufficient support in the country to deem the consumption of alcoholic beverages was detrimental to the health of citizens and/or morally sinful. However, as human behavior demonstrates, there were enough people who wished to continue to consume alcoholic beverages and the prohibition laws were too difficult to enforce. Consequently, the twenty-first amendment restored their right to drink.

This is an excellent example of democracy in action. As revealed by the process, the majority of people prevailed and subsequently invoked their right to natural law.

The process followed wasn't in error. In fact, it was the appropriate way of trying to restrict human behavior for the perceived good of society. Although the public's ability to produce and distribute alcoholic beverages was addressed by the 18th and 21st amendments, issues regarding public safety, etc. are not totally determined by adopting or repealing a constitutional amendment. Instead, there are other governmental avenues to monitor human behavior in a social environment. Various moral, legal, and safety issues are addressed in numerous court decisions, legislative regulations, and executive decrees and edicts.

Hence, institutional law does indeed come into play and takes precedence over natural law when it's determined the activity which people prefer to follow interferes with or harms society as a whole and the citizens are no longer safe. Such is the case whenever institutional government puts meaningful restrictions on personal behavior. For example, this is seen with the laws regulating the use of an automobile. Prospective operators must first take a driving test before they're issued a license to operate a motor vehicle. Speed limits are set and enforced to control the reckless behavior of driving where innocent people are at risk to be injured or killed. Likewise, there are rules regarding the incarceration of drivers who end up killing someone while driving while under the influence of alcohol, as measured by breathalyzer and blood-alcohol tests. Additional controls are put in place for the sellers of alcoholic beverages, i.e. bartenders, who are legally responsible if a customer gets inebriated in his bar and then drives a vehicle that's involved in an accident.

Furthermore, the consumption of stimulants or depressants that would cause the person under their influence to either commit a crime or allow themselves to be easy victims of a crime is restricted by institutional government's regulations when necessary. Similarly, such is the case for the use of highly addictive, illegal drugs such as cocaine and heroin. Where the use of such drugs put people's lives in jeopardy, it's the responsibility of the institutional government to prohibit the distribution and use of these drugs in order to protect the community at large.

Every person has to make the right decisions in life. When the right decisions are made, then the individual is basically worthy of his or her existence. Perhaps more obvious, a person who lives by a set of moral values and holds a positive outlook on life is worthy of the country and way of life that he acquired from the nation's founders.

Our Model Nation

Crime and Punishment

CRIME IN AMERICA MUST be punished. The country has become compromised to an appreciable extent on crime and its punishment, for people aren't held as accountable for their actions as they should be. It doesn't matter if the crime is civil or criminal. It covers all acts of transgressions including the so-called white collar crimes as well as those of a criminal nature where people are victimized in emotional and physical ways. Whenever crime is committed to harm others then the perpetrators, if convicted in a court of law, must be held accountable and properly punished.

The problem stems from the moral standards of each citizen as well as society as a whole. Raise the moral standards of the people and we can reduce the level of crime. A leveling off of personal accountability has occurred in this country. The pendulum has swung from the strict ethical control and public embarrassment punishment, which was typical of the Puritan society, to the modern day social structure characterized by suspended sentences, time off for good behavior, and a lessening of penalties for the more serious crimes.

We've taken a more lenient approach as far as the prevention and punishment of criminal offenses go. The crimes have never changed, but somehow the punishment and general opinion on the maliciousness of certain crimes have. We mustn't let the motive of the offender overshadow the brutality of the deed. Instead, the focus should be on the actual viciousness of the crime and the harm that occurs to the victim, along with a definitive compensation for his or her loss.

Part of the reason why the situation has changed over the years is because of amnesty groups and other advocates of pardoning and forgiveness that have come to the forefront in the criminal justice system. Emphasis is often placed on the environment in which the offender is raised, and if he or she was the victim of crime. Typically, these advocacy groups have focused on the perpetrator of the crime as a wronged human being who has made mistakes.

Irrespective of one's background, crime does occur because of a willingness to break the law. This includes the desire to take another person's property or steal his money. It also includes the lack of remorse for physically harming or even killing another individual. Along those lines, capital punishment should be administered for the more heinous crimes against society such as mass murder of citizens, or the killing of police officers, firemen, and ambulance personnel.

It's worthwhile to evaluate the categories of all criminal acts, from misdemeanors to felonies, alongside their corresponding lists of retributions, from house arrest to capital punishment. The goal is to make sure the punishment fits the crime, such that the punishment applied is neither too lenient nor too harsh. Any correlation between crime and retribution must be timely, reasonable, and just. It must be applied equally to everyone, and it's up to society as a whole to determine the criteria used to establish the proper balance.

Part of the punishment regiment should include having the incarcerated individuals contribute to the welfare of society by being given work assignments to complete on a regular basis.

By choosing to commit a crime, the individuals forfeit personal rights and social benefits. Those convicted of felonies surrender their right to privacy, to bear arms, to vote, to secure certain employment opportunities, and so forth. While incarcerated, it's expected the individuals earn their way back into a free and open society by serving the sentence imposed on them in a court of law, by performing the duties assigned, and by displaying redemptive-type behavior.

As indicated, there are some crimes so severe they require capital punishment, or life in prison with no opportunity for parole. Nonetheless, there should be the opportunity for offenders to be rehabilitated and given a second chance if the offense falls outside the most grievous categories. It depends on the severity of the crime and the circumstances which brought it about. Once a proper punishment vs. crime matrix is structured by society, issues that deal with making reasonable adjustments to the rehabilitation process can be resolved. These involve dealing with the questions of plea bargaining, sentence reduction, time off for good behavior, visitation privileges, amenities while incarcerated, and so forth. Following such a review, recommendations can be made.

As previously noted, the best approach to preventing acts of crime is to improve the social norms through education in the home, at school, and in the church. This must begin early in life and continue throughout childhood and the teenage years. The moral values people are taught as children, the positive role models they have in life, and the fact they must be held accountable for mistakes made out of bad behavior or evil intent are issues that need to be addressed. If that is done, then the level of crime should drop.

Our Model Nation

Americans Relationship to Their Government

THE PEOPLE OF THIS country must never forget that the government is theirs. We live in a republic known as the United States of America, with a federal system of government and a constitution. Ours is a representative democracy. It is a government of the people, by the people, and for the people. The government and people are one.

All citizens are entitled to their opinions. They are free to question the direction the country is heading on various social, economic, and political issues. They're free to criticize policy decisions made by their elected representatives.

Though the citizens may be fearful of a centralized government that's afforded too much power, they can prevent it from happening by retaining a measurable level of power unto themselves. They can do this through the electoral process. This means they can elect representatives who support their political and socio-economic views, and in doing so replace the officials who don't. Hence the people shouldn't fear government; rather they should challenge themselves to participate in the political process. What's important is the moral fiber and political fortitude of the American public. That determines the state of the union, not the audacity of its political leaders.

Our Model Nation

American Heritage

Every nation's history is important because it informs the current generation of people where it came from and what previous generations endured to arrive at where the country is today. Whether it contains good or bad information, it's necessary to retain a comprehensive record of our American heritage because a careful and honest review can provide the insight and knowledge needed to correct past errors and promote previous successes.

The strength and perseverance of the American way of life is enshrined in its recorded history, and as such is passed down from one generation to the next as heritage. American heritage then is a museum where we're able to preserve the positive achievements of American life. Additionally, it is a library where we can read about the social, economic, and political advances that made this country great.

However American heritage is more than museums and libraries. It is also an active part of American life which continues to grow and develop. Indeed, the basis for the growth and development of American heritage is a classroom where a child learns about his country and pledges allegiance to its flag. It's a home where a child resides with his family and understands why he pledges to the flag. And it's a church where a child freely worships God, in whose belief an assemblage of people were inspired to install the flag as the symbol of the American adventure, established with liberty and justice for all.

Our Model Nation

Threats of Aggression and Tyranny

IT SEEMS THAT AMERICA, as every great country that holds a definitive place in history, has always had to face crises that threatened its social-economic, religious, and governmental institutions. Indeed, these are crises that threatened its very existence.

We may owe little to ourselves but we owe a tremendous amount of gratitude to those who fought and died in the defense of this country. We owe something to the doughboys of World War I, the G.I.s of World War II, the men of Korea, the rangers of Viet Nam, and the soldiers of Iraq and Afghanistan. We owe something to them for they have fought tyranny and came home physically wounded and emotionally drained. Many have given their lives. They died fighting aggression, while standing as champions for freedom and justice.

Not only do we owe thanks to past veterans, but we owe it to members of the armed forces who currently serve and protect us. The members of the U.S. armed forces are the guardians of liberty for they protect our country and carry out the military missions required to defeat our enemies. They deserve our total support as they're the ones who ensure that the American way of life is guaranteed for our children and grandchildren.

Who are the enemies we're referring to? The enemies are and always have been military, religious, economic, and social antagonists. Since the beginning of civilization, nation after nation has challenged one another over the differences of competing ideologies.

Why should our country have such enemies and why must we fight off the threat of constant aggression? We assume that

America's role in world affairs is always based upon what's right, while its enemy's role is based on what's wrong. If this is true, then America should never be tempted to engage in an unjust position in an unfair war, a war wherein we choose not to fight for those who are oppressed and striving to secure liberty for themselves. Hence, we would never join an unjust cause and no American soldier will die in vain.

It's our responsibility to ensure that America, as a nation, always stands on the side of righteousness. To guarantee this, we must continue to monitor our values and principles in order to correct any shortcomings that may arise. Then any war we engage in can be done so without hesitation. The world's consciousness will know in advance that the American people would be justified in engaging in combat. And Americans wouldn't second guess their actions, rather they will strike hard and fast to win because they're dedicated to champion liberty and repel tyranny.

Relative to sustaining our way of life, we might ask how strong is our commitment? Is today's American more dedicated to the principles of freedom than the American of the1770s who fought the British during the American Revolution? Is today's American more interested in preserving the union than the American of the early 1860's who fought the Civil War? Likewise, is today's American more careful to protect his country than he was on December 7, 1941 when Pearl Harbor was bombed? And we ask, is today's American more on guard than he was on September 11, 2001 when the World Trade Center was leveled? For sure, we've been unwavering in our commitment to preserve this nation.

As we know, people cannot live forever so they strive to develop a country that will. The early founders of America were no exception. To attain those ends the founding fathers endorsed the basic freedoms of speech, religion, and press. They established the basic rights to bear arms and to a speedy and public trial in either criminal or civil matters. And they afforded the basic protection of property, as well as protection from unreasonable search and seizure, or from excessive bail, fines, and punishment.

Hence, the American Revolution was fought to establish a nation of people dedicated to the preservation of individual life, liberty, and the pursuit of happiness. This country paid a harsh price for its freedom and the aforesaid principles in the number of lives lost during the Revolutionary War.

In 1775 at Concord, Massachusetts, the American colonists fired shots for liberty that were heard around the world. They were among the first contingents of citizen-soldiers to pick up arms in order to defend their homeland. The encounter represents the beginning of the Revolutionary War, wherein the American people battled a foreign power over the control of their destiny. Their goal was to eliminate unfair taxation and economic exploitation, as they attempted to gain control of their lives and establish a republic of and by the people. With the establishment of the United States of America under a new constitution, the inherent right to pursue a life of opportunity based on equality and justice was bestowed upon its citizens. The enemy was the British Empire, the foreign power that delivered a high percentage of the early settlers to America.

This country faced another crisis in the Civil War of 1860 to 1864. It stood as a soul-searching test to define the socio-economic system under which we would live. We were divided into two camps which desired to live under systems that were incompatible with one another relative to personal liberties, human morality, and the acceptable means of earning a living.

Importantly, the outcome of the war resulted in the adoption of the 13th, 14th, and 15th amendments to the constitution which affirmed that the fundamental principles of freedom, citizenship, and right to vote, on which the nation was founded did apply to all regardless of race, color, or prior status of servitude.

The future the nation was aptly expressed by President Lincoln in his Gettysburg Address of 1863 when he stated that "government of the people, by the people, for the people, shall not perish from the earth". In the War Between the States, the nation paid a heavy price to extend freedom, opportunity, and equality to all members of society. The enemy of the Civil War was our self.

As with all wars, this nation paid dearly for its existence during the two major world conflicts of the twentieth century. In World Wars I and II, this country paid a high price for the protection of personal liberties and freedom as it pertained to a multitude of countries across the face of the earth. Our enemies during World War I and II were fascism and imperialism as exemplified by the early and mid-twentieth century political-military powers of Germany, Italy, and Japan. We and our allies succeeded. Freedom again was saved for the world in general and for the western nations of Europe in particular.

During the twentieth century, the two major adversaries of America have been the Nazi war machine and communism. They were our economic and military antagonists. Since the fall of the Soviet Union, there's been a reduction in the immediate threat of communism to the American way of life. However, communism is alive and well in Russia and China as well as several smaller countries such as North Korea, Cuba, and Vietnam.

Regarding the nature of our adversaries over the years, is there any difference in how committed they were to destroying our society? Were the communists of the latter part of the 1900s more deceitful than the Germans and Japanese of World War II? Are the terrorists of today more ruthless that the communists of the latter part of the 1900s? Throughout American history, the answer is . . . our enemies have been equally dedicated to causing us harm.

On September 11, 2001, a direct and fearful strike was delivered by foreign terrorists against the American society. For sure, the enemies of today are radical religious zealots. Their weapons of choice and capability are acts of terrorism. Once again, America is called upon to take up arms and destroy this latest challenge to personal freedom.

Throughout all the conflicts we've faced, American men and women came to the aid of their country. They've sacrificed their time, and in many cases their lives, for the preservation of the nation.

Again, we may not owe anything to ourselves. But for sure, we owe everything to the welfare of our children and grandchildren.

We must continue on and fight the current enemies of fairness and justice, and the American way of life.

America will prevail. Whenever great leaders are called upon to solve the great problems of the day, they do so. The motivation to survive is based on our unwavering commitment to this land and the freedoms we enjoy. This involves our heritage, and the respect and pride we hold for country and self.

Our Model Nation

No Society or Government is Perfect

AS A PEOPLE, AMERICANS have certain values and beliefs as well as specific likes and dislikes they live by. They have a cultural identity that spans political, religious, and social disciplines. Because America offers its land and resources as a place for the preservation of life, liberty, and the pursuit of happiness, it doesn't mean that it is a "perfect" society.

Nor does it mean America's persona is untarnishable. The American citizens are not symbols of human flawlessness; rather, they are ordinary people going about their daily lives. This land may be beautiful and its government may afford individual liberties and freedoms, but the American people are not indifferent nor unbiased. Many have strong feeling about the "correct" manner by which people should be governed. For example, there are those who believe that full economic support from the government should be provided to everyone regardless of a person's status of citizenship or situation of employment. However, an open and progressive culture doesn't necessarily make a perfect society.

The majority of the American people believe in God and at one time Bible reading and prayer were permitted in school classrooms. However, in the early 1960s lawsuits charged this was an infringement upon the right of freedom from religion. It was argued, if the United States was a country of true individual rights and freedoms, then no school child should be subjected to the teachings of religion in a public school. Indeed, the Supreme Court upheld separation of church and state precepts and the American people lost the ability to pray together and conduct Bible reading in a public school setting. But court rulings on the appropriateness and legality of public religious expressions don't make for a perfect society.

Furthermore, the American people have faced an aggressive, foreign enemy for several decades in the form of communism. The communists believe in a socialistic society with a totalitarian type government, whereas the United States has supported a free enterprise or capitalistic system with a democratic form of government. Irrespective of these competing socio-economic designs, the Communist party is permitted to function in the United States. This is because America is held as a land where everyone and anyone can express themselves and live as free, unencumbered members of society. Yet tolerance of social and political disparity within one's borders doesn't make a perfect society.

The American people realize there are limits to living in a social environment. Along with the rights and freedoms, there comes a corresponding set of responsibilities and obligations from the citizens. No society is "perfect" and no government is "perfect". What works best is to have the proper balance regarding rights and responsibilities. The people and government have to decide which individual freedoms are protected and which individual liberties are partially or wholly surrendered for the welfare of the state. Just as there are opportunities for freedom and individual liberties that must be upheld, there are corresponding responsibilities and requirements that individual citizens must meet in support of the nation and its government.

Americans must reaffirm their identity and declare who they are, what they stand for, and what they believe in. They should delineate the design and objectives of their institutions of family, employment, education, religion, and so forth. With the institutions of American life thusly defined, any citizen who forcibly transgresses against those institutions should be properly accused and judged in a court of law. And because government is one such institution, any adversary who attempts to undermine and destroy the government of the United States must be swiftly brought to justice.

Our Model Nation

Presidents

IN THE LATE 1700s and early 1800s, great leaders became presidents. That's the perception generations of Americans have held regarding the founding fathers who went on to become president. Throughout the years, each generation had direct knowledge of its presidents; and to the extent possible, each generation was aware of its presidents' strengths and weaknesses as well as their personality and moral character. Even though several presidents haven't necessarily been considered great leaders once in office, most presidents in times of crises have displayed the ability to make great decisions for the benefit of the country.

Our Model Nation

President Kennedy

As STATED IN THE Declaration of Independence, "When in the course of human events, it becomes necessary . . . ". On Friday, November 22, 1963, President John F. Kennedy was killed by an assassin's bullet in Dallas, Texas. On Monday, November 25, at the President's funeral in Arlington National Cemetery a twenty-one gun salute was given. Mr. Kennedy heard neither the crack of the sniper's rifle in the midst of an excited and friendly Dallas crowd, nor the thunderous roar of the artillery volleys as a mournful nation saluted its lost leader.

The shot that killed the President is surely a shot heard round the world. On Friday, November 22, it became necessary for this nation to recommit itself to protect and defend the freedoms afforded to us, and to combat evilness whenever it challenges our way of life.

Our Model Nation

Capitol Plan

THE FOLLOWING PLAN DEALS with the relocation of key components of the legislative and executive branches of the U.S. government. The Capitol Plan has the potential to provide better security for numerous administrative offices and major departments of government, as well as create a permanent archival site to house the significant accomplishments of American life.

According to this plan, Washington, D.C. would remain as the seat of federal lawmaking for the legislative and judicial branches of government. That is, Congress and the Supreme Court would remain there. Their membership would stay the same as well for there would still be 435 representatives and 100 senators comprising Congress. Also, there would remain nine justices on the Supreme Court.

The executive branch would decentralize and leave Washington, D.C. to be distributed among the several states. Within the executive branch, the president and vice-president as well as their immediate staffs would remain in Washington, D.C. The rest of the executive branch, specifically the several cabinet departments, would be relocated to various states. Each cabinet secretary would maintain an office in Washington, D.C. as well as in the new, relocated department's headquarters.

In general the administration of the cabinet departments, as well as other independent executive agencies distributed among the several states, wouldn't be altered. It would just be a change of address. The executive branch could continue to undergo shifts in emphasis however. There may be the establishment of new departments and agencies as well as the elimination of others.

Also, the departments might experience adjustments as to their functional role in society.

The present U.S. capitol building would become basically a terminal to a new building complex that houses Congress and its staff offices. The new complex would be located across the Potomac River from Washington, D.C. It would be built in Arlington County, Virginia, on a hill at the end of a corridor that lies in an L-shaped line with the present capitol building. The corridor runs west, beginning at the U.S. capitol, and proceeds parallel to and within the area bounded by Constitution and Independence Avenues. It runs from the Capitol, through the Mall, the Washington Monument, the reflecting pool, Lincoln Memorial, and across the Potomac River. The corridor then turns northwest of Arlington National Cemetery to a hilltop in Arlington County between the George Washington Memorial Parkway and Arlington Boulevard.

The present capitol building would be preserved as a historical site and national museum. The current representative and senate chambers would be open to the public similar to the way the Rotunda and Statuary Hall are now open. There would be several monorail and subway passageways, above and below ground, that connect the city terminal, i.e., the Capitol, to the new legislative building complex. There would be monorail trains specific for the congressmen and governmental employees which originate at the current Senate building. Likewise, there would be monorail trains for the general public which begin at the House of Representatives. Also, there would be subway trains that access a series of underground archives, including a records and files center, a library, and a museum.

The new legislative building complex, located in Virginia, would be for government work only. Strict security measures would be enforced relative to access to and the operation of the new legislative buildings. Other than a cafeteria, post office, and medical clinic there would be no gift shops, barber shops, banking facilities, and railroad or airline ticket outlets located in this new legislative complex. These shops and services, which are located in the present capitol building, would still be in use. The subways for the congressmen and government employees would terminate under the senate chamber. The subways for the general public and the archives, records and files center, etc. would terminate beneath the representative chamber. The members of Congress would continue to reside and pursue social activities in the city proper as well as in its suburbs.

As indicated, the Supreme Court would remain the same as it is now. Likewise, the White House would remain as the home and office of the president. The executive office building would remain in use.

Some may feel that it's unnecessary to move the offices of the congressmen and legislative chambers from Capitol Hill. It can be cited that Statuary Hall served as the headquarters for the House of Representatives for fifty years prior to 1857. It has since been converted into a public assembly area where each state was given the opportunity to exhibit two statues of their prominent statesmen. Likewise, the Senate met in the old senate chambers of the Capitol for forty-nine years before moving to its present location in 1859. From 1860 to 1935, the Supreme Court occupied this same old senate chamber.

Relocations such as these took place because the original facilities were no longer adequate for the legislative and judicial bodies of government. If and when this becomes the case for the representatives and senators who meet in the current capitol building, this plan ought to be considered. The plan possibly could take from several years to decades to complete. It would take as long, at least, as the rate of materials, labor, and finances would permit.

A major feature of the capitol plan is to provide for a permanent location to preserve records of American heritage and culture. All important aspects of American life ranging from government to religion, economics to employment, and health care to education, etc. would be retained. The records would be stored in the secure, underground vaults beneath the Mall between the capitol building and the Lincoln Memorial.

Should the plan to relocate congressional lawmakers to the new site in Arlington County, Virginia not go forward, the nation could still proceed with the proposal to create a new and lasting archival site beneath the Mall. The subway tunnels and storage vaults could be constructed and thereby used to preserve our historical records.

Our Model Nation

Decentralization of the Executive

THIS PORTION OF THE plan is directed at relocating the executive departments of government to designated individual states. Examples of where the departments might go are given below.

The Department of State could be located in the State of Florida. All central offices and administrative work conducted by the State Department would relocate there. All State Department transactions with foreign nations would be conducted at a new building complex. Foreign embassies and offices would be moved into this complex area as well. Airlines and ocean vessels carrying ambassadors and diplomats conducting state department business would arrive and leave via Florida.

The headquarters for all foreign organizations and alliances, which involve foreign nations and our country, would be moved outside the continental United States, say to Puerto Rico. If this isn't possible, then these organizations should be located in Florida. Thus, preferably the United Nations and the Organization of American States could be moved outside continental United States, or relocated to Florida.

Besides the actual federal government complex, there will be a national museum about the State Department located in Florida. This museum-library complex would be open to all citizens of the United States and would preserve documents and other materials pertaining to the history of the U.S. State Department. There would also be a reception-recreational center located next to the museum-library. The reception-recreational center would contain the reception, dining, theater, and recreation facilities that are necessary to the personnel of the State Department. Further, these facilities would be available to the populace of Florida as well as to all American citizens. The State Department's office buildings would be built, financed, and staffed by the federal government. If approved by the residents of Florida, the Department of State's museum-library and the adjoining reception-recreational center would be built, financed, and staffed by the State of Florida. Because the State Department would be located in their state, it's anticipated that Floridians would be supportive and proud that their state is the home of the foreign affairs sector of American life.

The Department of Treasury could be located in the state of Virginia. A new building complex for the Department of Treasury would be built. All major mints and vaults would be located in Virginia. All money, paper and coin, would be printed or minted in Virginia. The administration of all treasury agencies located throughout the United States would originate in Virginia. The new building project of the U.S. Treasury would be built, financed, and staffed by the federal government of Washington, D.C. If approved by the people of Virginia, the national museum-library on the history of the U.S. Treasury Department would be built, financed, and staffed by the State of Virginia. The adjoining reception-recreational center would also be built and maintained by the State of Virginia. Hopefully, the citizens of Virginia would take pride their state represents and preserves the system of monetary exchange for the United States.

The Department of Defense could be located in the state of California. It would be in California where the offices of the Pentagon would relocate. A new building complex for the Department of Defense would be built and all major military and defense offices would be stationed there. The military bases and naval installations throughout the United States would remain in their respective states as part of the defense system. The headquarters for defense, however, would be located in California. This new defense headquarters would be built, financed, and staffed by the federal government. Again, if approved by the citizens of California, the national museum-library on the history of the Defense Department would be built, financed, and staffed by the state of California. The reception-recreational center would likewise be built and main-tained by California. Presumably, the people of California would be proud their state represents the home of air, land, and sea defense capabilities for the United States of America.

The Department of Justice could be located in Massachusetts, the Department of Interior in Wyoming, and the Department of Agriculture in Iowa. The Department of Commerce could be es-tablished in New York, the Department of Labor in Michigan, and the Department of Health and Human Services in Maryland.

The Department of Housing and Urban Development could be established in New Hampshire. The Department of Transpor-tation could be established in Oklahoma and the Department of Energy could be located in Texas. The Department of Education could be located in Pennsylvania, the Department of Veterans Af-fairs in South Dakota, and the Department of Homeland Security in Louisiana. Regarding Homeland Security, a couple of other states such as New York and California could have immigration offices, but the headquarters for immigration and naturalization would be located in the Department of Homeland Security's com-plex in Louisiana. Most immigration to the United States would come through Louisiana.

In regard to the "home" of several additional independent and semi-independent agencies of government, the Environmen-tal Protection Agency could be part of the Department of Interior or Department of Health and Human Services. The Central Intel-ligence Agency could become a part of the Department of Justice or Department of Defense. The Federal Reserve System could be added to the Department of Treasury, and Amtrak would logically be a part of the Department of Transportation.

Along with other government sponsored broadcasting and publishing networks, the Post Office agency could be located in a newly created Department of Communication.

As described for the Departments of State, Treasury, and Defense, each executive department would have a building com-plex in its respective state that would house a national museum-library that delineates the state's executive responsibilities, and a reception-recreational center for conference and entertainment functions.

Each cabinet department would generate two complete sets of records. One set would be held at the museum, library, and archive complex located within each department's respective state. It'll be in the form of displays, models, records, books, sound-tapes, films, video-tapes, DVD discs, electronic recordings, etc. The second set of records would be stored in the underground vaults beneath the Mall in Washington, D.C.

A benefit to having the departments of the executive branch of government and their administrative offices spread out across the United States is that the entire federal government wouldn't be crippled if a foreign country launched a major military attack on Washington, D.C.

It's anticipated the decentralization of the executive branch of government would help build support for key areas of American life. By having government's responsibility for important aspects of societal life distributed across a variety of states, it is expected public awareness will expand and greater participation by the citizenry in public-sponsored events will occur. Additionally, it's likely an individual's pride in country and dedication to its institutions would grow if a particular focal point of societal life was housed in the person's home state.

Our Model Nation

*Future Design of Society
and Government's Role*

THIS PROPOSAL DEALS WITH establishing several universal institutions of social living in America, all of which currently exist in various stages of development. Some are well-established and highly organized, whereas others are less established and less formal. Some have existed since the beginning of human history. The proposed universal institutions of society are family, government, religion, employment, education, health care, recreation, communication, transportation, financial resources, utilities-services, energy, ecology, environment, and discovery. These institutions are described in depth in *A Pen Named Man: Our Destiny*. Similar to the proposal on the decentralization of departments of the executive branch of government, the administrative bodies of these major institutions would be distributed across the country, located in separate states.

Outlines of two of the proposed universal institutions of social living are given below. These are the institutions of employment and discovery.

The social-economic employment institution would consist of an association of businesses and industries aligned together to meet the subsistence needs of the citizens. No business or industry would be required to join this system; rather, it would be based on voluntary enrollment. The level of involvement of a business or industry is likewise optional. Further, no individual is required to participate in the program and the degree of involvement can vary according to his or her wishes.

The restructured employment system would call for awarding equal or comparable benefits to employees that are based upon equal or comparable work performed. It'll be designed so any individual who is willing to work will have an available job. He or she will be working in an occupation that manufactures a product or performs a service that's useful to society at large. The compensation for employment will be the basic necessities of life which include allotments for living quarters, food, and clothing. There will be the supplemental necessities of education and health care available, as well as the access to broad-based recreation facilities. Additional amenities include credit towards transportation, communication, utility-services, and energy.

Every person would be appropriately rewarded for his industriousness and corresponding contributions to society. A participating individual would be entitled to the necessities of life on a fair and equitable basis, if he or she satisfies the required work assignments. Not only should life's necessities be available to anyone who's willing to work, importantly they would be guaranteed to anyone who actually does work to earn them. These represent basic entitlements to people who are committed to living and working together.

A key benefit of a restructured employment system is that life's necessities will also be provided to people who are incapable of working because of mental or physical limitations. Indeed, the restructured social-economic system is designed so an individual contributes to the welfare of less fortunate people as he participates in his everyday work routine. Hence, the individual doesn't contribute once in a while as he would by contributing to an auxiliary, charitable-type organization. Rather, a person is positioned to contribute every day of his working life, if his place of employment is geared toward advancing society's overall "quality of life".

The restructured social-economic employment institution would function independently of the government of the United States. It would be governed by an administrative board comprised of managers chosen from the participating businesses and industries. The members to the administrative board would be elected to serve for specified term lengths.

The administrative board's role is to manage business operations as well as employee performance, and to ensure the work performed serves the humanitarian interests of society. It's an administration that neither legislates nor judges the legalities of either its business or employee activities. Such judgments rightfully fall under the scope of the U.S. government.

The U.S. government in Washington, D.C. would oversee this program to the extent it doesn't allow inequities to exist within the operation of the employment institution's framework. Likewise, it ensures the socio-economic employment institution's external performance isn't unduly influenced by other institutions of society such as health care, education, religion, or even government itself. The government would make sure that laws aren't breached under the operation or administration of the restructured employment institution.

The separate branches of government would continue to perform their legislative, executive, and judicial duties as defined by the U.S. constitution. The federal government would guarantee that the rights of the citizens are upheld and criminal and civil transgressions are addressed. When crimes are committed, it's the responsibility of government to ensure the perpetrators are apprehended and then promptly and fairly tried in a court of law.

An important outcome of a restructured employment system would be that the needs of people are met and society as a whole moves forward. Advantages are not only in meeting the physiological needs of people, but also satisfying their psychological requirements through the establishment of the institutions of health care, education, recreation, etc.

The universal institution of discovery would consist of a nation-wide association of research organizations dedicated to the study of all sciences. The discovery institution would focus on the natural sciences of biology, chemistry, and physics. It would include the study of animal life and botany. It would cover the areas of earth science, astronomy, and space exploration. Further, the discovery institution would be dedicated to the social sciences as well. This includes sociology, psychology, and philosophy. It also covers ethics, law, and political science.

As with employment, the institution of discovery would be governed by an administrative board comprised of managers chosen from participating research and development entities.

The institution of discovery would compile information from all places of higher learning. It would collect and distribute data derived from research labs located at manufacturing and industrial sites, schools and universities, as well as medical centers and hospitals. The institution would ensure that knowledge gained through research and development is secured. To do this, the institution would establish archive centers to preserve the major advancements gleamed through discovery.

The archival centers of the institution of discovery would play an important role relative to recording and maintaining the American heritage. Similar to the proposal for each cabinet department of the executive branch of government, every major institution of society would have individual libraries and museums dedicated to preserving its legacy.

As with the executive branch of government, each universal institution would maintain two complete sets of records. One set will be held at the central museum, library, and archive building of each respective institution. The second set will be stored beneath the Mall at the Washington, D.C. site.

Each major universal institution, such as education, health care, communication, transportation, etc., will have a program or display that's representative of the duties and operations of the institution. Every month the exhibit of each institution will tour the United States and display the history or heritage of the particular institution in a different state. The exhibition will be held in the theaters of the other institutions' recreation centers. The citizens won't be charged a fee to attend these "traveling" exhibitions. An institution's exhibit could tour twelve states per year, so each state would present the updated exposition of a specific institution a little more than once every four years. Every institution would have its own company of presenters and lecturers to tour the states.

The construction and operation of the central facilities of each major institution will take place via the people working within the universal social-economic, employment institution. Member companies, which are involved in the building and trades industry, will provide the materials and workforce. The nationwide construction of the libraries and museums would likewise include the efforts of college students, prisoners, and private concerns.

The convicts in prisons would participate in building these nationwide projects. They would be put to work laying the buildings' foundation and other construction work. Thus, not only would the criminals' work assignments pay back the taxpayers who fund their incarceration, but the program would also create an opportunity for the criminals to perform a service that's beneficial to society. Hopefully, the prospect of criminals being forced to do manual labor would provide an incentive to not break the law and thereby help reduce the overall crime rate in America.

It should be also noted that a reorganization of the educational system in this country could guarantee that all young people who desire to attend college will be able to do it. Each college student, who cannot pay for his education, can finance it by working in a national museum or library while he goes to school. He could similarly pay for college expenses by being employed on a part-time basis in the universal employment institution, or any other major institution such as health care, communication, transportation, utilities-service, and energy.

The plan for national museums and libraries could provide jobs for elderly people as well. Say, in the early sixties of one's life, a person retires from his regular place of employment and begins working at a library or national museum. The number of hours a person works depends on several factors. The factors include the number of individuals who want to work and the number of national museum jobs that are available. Factors also include the interests of the employee, his age, and health status. Health permitting, the job would be available for as long as the senior citizen wanted it.

Thus, this plan would provide semi-retired citizens the opportunity to be employed in a profession that advances the quality of societal life. Senior citizens aren't required to join this project. Those individuals who are financially secure, or have other interests, need not join. The program would proceed at the rate that the materials, finances, and manpower allow.

Some of the advantages of this program are listed below:

It would give college students the chance to work in a jobs-based program that allows them to continue their education regardless of financial status.

It would allow semi-retired senior citizens the opportunity to work and contribute, yet enjoy a significant amount of free time to pursue other interests in life.

It would provide an occupation well into old age for those people who want to participate.

It would force criminals and convicts to be contributing members of society.

It further represents the opportunity for people to participate in a program whereby they can maintain a careful and complete history of the advancements made in social living.

It would inspire a sense of pride in the citizens of a state, relative to the particular institution or cabinet department that's headquartered within the state.

It would provide instructorship and entertainment to the general public through the lectures and tour programs about the respective institutions of American life.

Hence, a person has many opportunities in life. Either you do something and make a difference, or you do nothing. Working together to improve societal life is a worthwhile goal and all Americans ought to be encouraged to pursue this calling at the national level.

Note the proposals and plans presented here are suggestions. The decision to implement or not implement them would be made by federal lawmakers in conjunction with state legislators, or by the will of the citizens through their voting preferences.